Science, Technology, and Government

Science, Technology, and Government

Murray N. Rothbard

Preface by
David Gordon

Mises Institute
Auburn, Alabama

March 1959. Previously unpublished.
First online edition 2004 by the Mises Institute.
2015 edition has been edited for typos only.

Mises Institute
518 West Magnolia Avenue
Auburn, Ala. 36832
mises.org

ISBN: 978-1-61016-639-3
ISBN Large Print Edition: 978-1-61016-648-5
ISBN epub: 978-1-61016-638-6

Contents

Preface

When Murray Rothbard wrote "Science, Technology, and Government" in 1959, supporters of the free market needed to confront a challenge that remains relevant today. In 1957, the Soviet Union launched its "Sputnik" satellite, thereby defeating the United States in the race between the two countries to be first into space. Did this victory show, or at least suggest, the superiority of Soviet centrally-planned science to the American market economy? Critics of the free enterprise system like John Kenneth Galbraith (one of Rothbard's least favorite economists) claimed that scientific research and development required government planning and control. The free market, these critics claimed, could not carry out the vast efforts research now required. Could private enterprise have built the atomic bomb? The Soviets have long since departed, but the fallacies in the arguments for centrally-controlled science live on today. Government spending on science and technology has increased far beyond its level in 1959.

In this brilliant monograph, Rothbard deftly turns the tables on the supporters of big government. In doing so, he displays his unique combination of mastery of theoretical principles and commanding knowledge of the empirical evidence and scholarly literature on every subject he addresses. He shows that science best advances under the free market: the claims to the contrary of the centralizers are spurious.

He begins with a fundamental question: how do we decide how much money to spend on research. The more we spend, the less we have to spend on other things. The decision is best left to the free market:

> This fact of reality, then, must be faced: if there are to be more scientists, or more scientific research, then there must be less people and less resources available for producing all the other goods and services of

> the economy. The crucial question, then, is: how much? How many people and how much capital are to be funneled into each of the various occupations, including science and technology? One of the great, if often unsung, merits of the free enterprise economy is that it alone can insure a smooth, rational distribution and allocation of productive resources. Through the free price systems, consumers signal laborers, capitalists, and businessmen on which occupations are most urgently needed, and the intricate, automatic workings of the price system convey these messages to everyone, thereby creating an efficient, smoothly working economy. (p. 16)

If an objector says to this, "But hasn't the free market, which you praise, resulted in a shortage of scientists?", Rothbard has a devastating answer; What shortage?

> If then, there is a shortage of scientists, market salaries for scientists will significantly rise, relative to other occupations. But since they have not so risen, is there really a shortage for scientists? This question was itself scientifically investigated only recently ... since 1939, salaries of engineers relative to earnings of doctors,

> dentists and lawyers, have declined, and have also declined relative to manufacturing wage earners. Even the salaries of clergymen, pharmacists, and school teachers, rose relative to engineers in this period. How, then, can there be a shortage of engineers? (pp. 29–30)

Even if there is no shortage of scientists, though, does it not remain the case that in current conditions, advances in scientific knowledge require gargantuan efforts beyond the scope of the free market? Rothbard meets this dogma head on:

> The myth has arisen that government research is made necessary by our technological age, because only planned, directed, large-scale "team" research can produce important inventions of develop them properly. The day of the individual or small-scale inventor is supposedly over and done with. And the strong inference is that government, as potentially the "largest-scale" operator, must play a leading role in even non-military scientific research. This common myth has been completely exploded by the researches of John Jewkes, David Sawers, and Richard Stillerman in their highly important recent work. Taking sixty-one of

> the most important inventions of the twentieth century ... Jewkes et. al. found that more than half of these were the work of individual inventors—with the individuals working at their own directions, and with very limited resources. (p. 47)

Not even the building of the atomic bomb is an exception to the superiority of the free market to governmentally-controlled science.

> The fundamental atomic discoveries had been made by academic scientists working with simple equipment. One of the greatest of these scientists has commented: "we could not afford elaborate equipment, so we had to think." Furthermore, virtually the entire early work on atomic energy, up to the end of 1940, was financed by private foundations and universities. And the development of the bomb was, for peacetime purposes, an extremely wasteful process. (p. 85)

The alleged great achievements of Soviet science, including the much-vaunted Sputnik, failed to impress Rothbard:

> We have heard a great deal recently about the alleged glories of Soviet science, and

> about the necessity of the United States catching up with such wonders as sputniks. What is the real record of Soviet science? Professor [John R.] Baker, analyzing this record, shows that, at the beginnings of the Soviet Union, the old pre-revolutionary scientists continued to do well, largely because science was not yet under government planning. That came with the Second Five-Year Plan, in 1932. ... Government control of science, government planning of science, is bound to result in the politicization of science, the substitute of political goals and political criteria for scientific ones. Even pro-Soviet scientists have admitted that Soviet research is inferior to American, that basic, as contrasted to applied, research, is neglected; that there is too much red tape; that little fundamentally creative work has been done; and that science is unduly governed by political considerations—such as the political views of the scientist propounding any given theory. Scientists are shot for taking the view that happens to be in political disfavor. (pp. 71–72).

So far as Sputnik is concerned, "American satellites have far superior instrumentation, and are therefore much more important scientifically" (p. 75).

Given his opposition to governmentally-controlled science, it is no surprise that Rothbard thinks that the best course of action for government is to get out of the way of the creative activities of the free market. It should, for example, reduce taxes to the greatest extent possible. In this connection, Rothbard in a brilliant paragraph exposes a common fallacy:

> Contrary to common belief, a tax exemption is not simply equivalent to a government subsidy. For a subsidy mulcts taxpayers in order to give a special grant to the favored party. It thereby adds to the ratio of government activity in the economy, distorts productive resources, and multiplies the dangers of government control and repression. A tax exemption, or any other type of tax reduction, on the one hand, reduces the ratio of government to private action; it frees private energies and allows them to develop unhampered; it reduces the danger of government control and distortion of the economy. It is a step toward the free market and the free society, just as

> a government subsidy is a step away from the free society. (p. 101)

This essay was found among Rothbard's papers. But the exact circumstances under which it was written have not yet come to light. As readers will soon discover, it contains an astonishing wealth of insights.

David Gordon
Los Angeles, July 2015

1.
General Principles[1]

The crucial economic question, and one of the most important social questions, is the allocation of resources: where should the various and numerous productive factors: land, labor, or capital, be allocated, and how much of each type to each use? This is the "economic problem," and all social questions must deal with it.

The important question of American science and technology is also a problem of the allocation of resources. Thus: our expanding technology and productivity require a great many scientists, researchers, engineers, etc. It

[1][This paper was written by Murray N. Rothbard (1926–1995) on commission in 1959 but was not published until 2004 on mises.org. It is part of the Rothbard Archives, the Mises Institute, Auburn, Alabama. —Ed.]

also requires many different types of resources to be invested in research and development. But our economy also requires many, many other goods and services, and many other types of investment, all of which are essential to its smooth functioning. It requires, for example, transportation to move goods, production lines to manufacture them, telephone operators and repairmen to staff our giant communications network. It even requires paper manufacturers and paper distributors—for how can a modern economy—including a scientific research staff operate without paper? These are just some of the infinite number of goods and services that go to make up a functioning economy.

This fact of reality, then, must be faced: if there are to be more scientists, or more scientific research, then there must be less people and less resources available for producing all the other goods and services of the economy. The crucial question, then, is: how much? How many people and how much capital are to be funneled into each of the various occupations, including science and technology?

One of the great, if often unsung, merits of the free enterprise economy is that it alone can insure a smooth, rational distribution and allocation of productive resources. Through the free price systems, consumers signal laborers, capitalists, and businessmen on which occupations are most urgently needed, and the intricate, automatic workings of the price system convey these messages to everyone, thereby creating an efficient, smoothly working economy. There is one and only one alternative to voluntary directions under a free price system: and that is government dictation. And this dictation is not only bad because it violates the tradition of individual freedom and free enterprise on which American greatness is built; it is also bad because it is inevitably inefficient and self-destructive. For while government intervention can and does hamper the economic system in its job of satisfying consumer demand, it cannot force the economy to follow its own demands efficiently. For piecemeal government intervention can only disrupt an economy and defeat its own ends; while overall central planning, by destroying the price system, robs itself of the possibility of rational economic calculation. Lacking a free price system, it cannot ever satisfy the desires of either consumers or its own planners, for it will not be able to allocate the infinite number and types of labor and capital resources with any degree of efficiency.

There are other considerations: we must recognize, for example, that only a free market is compatible with the free choice by every man of his own occupation. A governmentally-run economy must entail government planning of labor as well as of other resources—which means, ultimately, that people must be told what jobs (and where) they can work and at what they cannot. If the free market is prevented from offering its voluntary inducements of higher wages in those occupations and areas that are most needed by the consumers, and thereby from shifting labor peacefully while permitting every man to work at the job he likes best, then government must dictate every man's type and place of work, and we must all become slaves of the State.

From a moral, political, constitutional, and economic point of view alike, therefore, the Republican Party is committed to the fostering and maintenance of a free economy in a free society. How is the ever-challenging problem of modern science and technology to be met within this framework?

2.
Two Basic Problems: General Research and Military Research

The problem of science and technology in our modern world is really a twofold one, and the two problems should be strictly separated, instead of confused as they now are in the public mind. Problem A is the general allocation of resources into science and technology, as compared to the other sectors of the economy. Problem B is the allocation of needed resources into the military sphere, specifically of military technology. The first problem is a general economic problem, the second a specifically military one. As to the first problem, the solution follows swiftly and easily from our general premises: it is solely the job of the free market economy. Any government meddling with this job can only distort and disrupt the economy, injure the efficient workings and development of science and technology, and substitute unwanted coercion for individual freedom.

What of Problem B, the allocation of resources between the Civilian and the Military? Here we must consider the general function of government in the military sphere. Granting to government the virtual monopoly of force, the American System has been to entrust the use of that force for defense of person and property to the government. Having a virtual monopoly of defense, the government taxes private citizens to the extent needed for their defense against enemies foreign and domestic. In the American System, domestic defense has been the function of states and localities; military defense against foreign countries, the job of the Federal government. The Federal government, therefore, sets its budget to attain a certain level that it desires for military defense, and military research and development is certainly part of that defense.

The allocation of resources to military purposes, then, is under the American System the job of the Federal government. And yet this does not simply end the matter. For the government has the responsibility: (1) of never forgetting that scarce resources are always being allocated, and therefore that what the military gains the civilian sector loses; and (2) of leaving, wherever possible, military matters in the hands of the private economy, both on grounds of maximizing economic freedom and of maximizing economic efficiency. The first is a mode of thinking to which any government bureaucrat, civilian or military, is uncongenial, and which he must learn: learn to realize that more military means less for the private economy, and to remember that the armed forces are a derivative, a dependent upon a strong and healthy civilian economy. Army tanks depend on sound and healthy iron and steel factories, tank manufactures, railroads to move them, etc., unless we are to have complete socialism—which we have seen cannot work either—the military must rely on a myriad of private goods and services in order for it to function (including paper!).

This brings us to the second responsibility; to leave as much of military affairs as possible in private hands. Thus, the government needs planes; who should manufacture them, private industry or government? Not only would government manufacture of aircraft be hopelessly inefficient by its very nature, it would also cut against the basis of American society. Far better, then, for the government to tax or borrow the funds with which to buy the military products of private enterprise, rather than to manufacture the goods itself.

This principle is largely recognized in the field of material production. Why, then, shouldn't it hold for military scientific research? Private research and development, contracted for with government funds, is a far better policy, from any angle, than direct government research. (See below, on the Hoover Commission Task Force agreement with this view.) This is the principle for the Republican Party to follow in the area of military technology. In short, government, even in the military sphere, should function only as a consumer rather than a producer, purchasing equipment and research produced by private firms. This is the most efficient method, as well as the one most consonant with free enterprise. And note: this applies only to military research and development; all non-military work should be purely in private hands, both as consumers and producers.

Another important consideration: to the extent that the government still considers it militarily vital to employ technicians itself rather than purchase the services of private firms, it should hire these personnel on the free labor market rather than conscript them. Pushing back the frontiers of science, discovering new products and new methods, requires free, untrammeled minds who delight in the work they do and get paid according to their value; the work cannot be done by men who are drafted into forced labor for a sum far below the worth of their product. Slaves might perhaps be useful for sweeping floors or digging ditches; they cannot be successfully used for creative work, requiring ability and originality. And this, of course, raises another question, as pointed out in the Cordiner Report to the Department of Defense: more and more, modern military forces in the nuclear age, depend upon the skills and creativity of trained technicians, rather than on untrained doughboys. Is it not then one of the requirements of the nuclear (and bacteriological) age that we scrap the draft as obsolete and rely on the eager voluntary services of skilled technicians hired at the market prices that they deserve?

In all these problems, there is another basic question that we should not overlook: isn't freedom, rather than coercion, not only the best way to spur efficiency and scientific advance, but also the way to show the peoples of the world (including the peoples of the Soviet bloc) that the American way of freedom can beat the Soviet way of coercion at any time and on any ground? If, on the contrary, we try to race with the Soviets by employing essentially Soviet methods, which ideology will come to look better to the peoples of the world? The more we stress free and voluntary methods in our competition with the Soviets, the more do we show that we believe our own speeches on the merits and glories of freedom; the more we rely on coercive or statist methods, the more do we undercut our own ideology, appear as hypocrites to the nations of the world, and thus contribute to the ultimate victory of the Soviet ideology.

3.
Specific Problems: The Alleged Shortage of Scientists

We now have at our command the general principles with which to approach our problems; we may now turn to some specific applications of these principles.

First, let us turn to the widely-trumpeted problem of a grave "shortage" of scientists, researchers, engineers, etc. It is widely asserted that the Federal government should subsidize scientific education in order to relieve this supposed "shortage." Now let us analyze this question more closely:

In the first place, a "shortage" of scientists is a general, rather than a military problem. The military can purchase the services of as many existing scientists (either as direct employees or as employees of private contractors) as it requires; the burden of shortage will then be felt by the civilian, rather than by the military, sector. Apart from this, if there really is a shortage of scientists, how can it be remedied? Not by government; government cannot manufacture one scientist; the scientists must enter this profession themselves.

Now, there are two sources of supply of scientists: (a) from adults who have left the profession and can be induced to reenter (e.g., ex-lady chemists who are now housewives); and (b) youngsters who are entering the profession for the first time. The (a) category can be induced to reenter in only one way: by paying them higher salaries, and thus attracting an influx. And the second category, in the final analysis, can only be stimulated in the same way: by higher salaries. Youngsters enter the scientific field for a blend of two reasons: a love of the work, and the expected salaries and job opportunities. The former cannot be increased by anyone except the young scientist himself (although more can be done via educational methods to awaken his interest—see below); only the salary factor can be increased by others. The way to increase the supply of scientists, then, is simply to increase the salaries of scientists, relative to other occupations. (If all salaries increase, then obviously there is little or no added incentive to enter science.)

It is already becoming apparent that Federal aid to scientific education, for example, is an improper and unsuccessful method of relieving a shortage of scientists. We have seen that any shortage must stem from the fact that scientific salaries are not higher than other occupations. Suppose, then, that the Federal government spends tax money to subsidize science students. What are the effects? The only thing it may accomplish is to create more students of science, who then find that, because of the increased supply, scientific salaries are not only not raised—they are even lower compared to other fields. The result can only be to drive more and more scientists out of the field and into others, and to discourage any further students from taking advantage of the subsidized program. In short, the ultimate result of Federal subsidies to science study can only be to aggravate the scientist shortage rather than alleviate it, for the crucial problem: salaries, is worsened rather than improved by this intervention. This is one of numerous examples of a government intervention, aiming to solve a certain problem, ending by not solving it but creating new problems needing cure. The original purpose of the intervention is completely frustrated. And, this, if the government then tries to sure the worsened shortage by still heavier doses of Federal aid the shortage will only be aggravated still more.

The key, then, is scientific salaries. And here we come to another important point: there can be no lasting shortage of any occupation on the free market, for if there is a shortage, it will be quickly revealed in higher salaries, and these salaries will do all that is humanly possible to alleviate the shortage rapidly by attracting new people into the field (and bringing back those who left the field). If more scientists are needed, then free-market salaries will rise and induce a greater supply. If they are needed specifically by the military, then the military may increase its salaries for scientists directly, or the private scientific firms on government contract can raise their preferred salaries. Such are the workings of the market. No particular Federal intervention can do anything more to increase the needed supply of scientists. Furthermore, only the free market can decide how much salaries need to be increased to stimulate a sufficient supply. No form of governmental wage-fixing can do the job. (If the military sets its wage, it can use the free-market wage as a guide.)

If then, there is a shortage of scientists, market salaries for scientists will significantly rise, relative to other occupations. But since they have not so risen, is there really a shortage for scientists? This question was itself scientifically investigated only recently, after much loose speculation on the subject, in a highly important study by Blank and Stigler, of the National Bureau of Economic Research.[2]

The authors found, for example, that, in the last eighty years, the number of chemists and engineers in the United States expanded by considerably more than 17 times as much as the total labor force. Hardly appears like a

---

[2]David M. Blank and George J. Stigler, *The Demand and Supply of Scientific Personnel* (New York: National Bureau of Economic Research, 1957).

shortage! But, more important, Blank and Stigler stress the point that the very concept of "shortage" makes little sense except in relation to price—in this case, the price for scientific services. A shortage means that demand for the labor is greater than its supply at current wage rates, so that the wage rate tends to rise. Yet, upon investigating recent earning trends, Blank and Stigler find that, since 1939, salaries of engineers relative to earnings of doctors, dentists and lawyers, have declined, and have also declined relative to manufacturing wage earners.[3] Even the salaries of clergymen, pharmacists, and school teachers, rose relative to engineers in this period. How, then, can there be a shortage of engineers?

Neither can it be said that this relative decline of salaries is due to some sort of "exploitation" of engineers by their employers. For Blank and Stigler found a great deal

[3]Engineers constitute the vast bulk of the technological professions. In 1950, there were over 540,000 engineers, and 82,000 chemists, with all the rest of the scientists: physicists, mathematicians, biologists, geologists, etc., (excluding medicine) totaling less than the number of chemists.

of mobility between jobs among engineer-employers. Thus, we must conclude that, in recent decades, far from there being a shortage, the supply of engineers has grown more rapidly than the demand for their services. Even in the years since 1950, when demand for scientific services grew suddenly due to the Korean War, increases in scientific salaries have been no larger than in other occupations, and, indeed they have once again been smaller since the end of the spurt of Korean War demand in 1952.

Possibly, a shortage has been felt in recent years in engineers in industries doing military work. A typical reason: the Air Force insists on a formal review of all salaries paid by its private contractors, and on justification given for all salary increases. This downward pressure on salaries had tended to cause a slight shortage of scientists doing war-work. The remedy for this is for the government to be willing to see technologists paid at their full market worth—otherwise it can only bring difficulties for national defense. But, again, this has not caused a general shortage of technologists; just a possible shortage in the defense contract industries.

These findings appear to be contradicted by the enormous growth in newspaper want-ads for engineers, which have seemed to reflect a great engineer shortage. But: (1) newspaper ads have been growing as a method of recruiting; and (2) nine-tenths of the advertising space have been taken by defense contact, rather than civilian, firms. Possible reasons are the lower salaries in war work, and, in particular, the fact that the recruitment costs of advertising are, for the military contract firms, fully reimbursed by the government.

In addition to their crucial studies of engineers and other scientists, Blank and Stigler also investigated the fields of mathematics and physics. These scientists are mostly on college and university facilities: 87 percent of mathematicians and almost 60 percent of physicists are employed in colleges. The authors found that the rapidly rising trend of college enrollments, coupled with the steady fall in faculty-to-student ratios in these subjects, insure a high and expanding demand for physics and mathematics professors far into the future. And as for supply, the growing increase in the relative, as well as absolute, number of Ph.D.'s in the sciences attests to the expanding supply. So there need be no fears of a general shortage of mathematicians or of physicists either.

There is another way in which government has tended to create its own shortage of scientists working on military projects. This is through onerous security and secrecy regulations that make working conditions unpleasant and unattractive to scientists. To be sure, we don't want to encourage Russian spies to steal our military secrets. And yet we must recognize that scientific invention is the discovery of natural laws, and that these laws are open to all to find, whether Russians or Americans. Throughout history, no important new invention has remained a secret for long, and either espionage or independent discovery would eventually yield the Russians the same technology. It is far more important, therefore, to create a climate of freedom in which scientists can operate creatively. And if scientists are naturally reluctant to work under onerous restrictions, the only way to induce them to give their free creative energies to military work is by relaxing these restrictions. And it must be conceded that, knowing the bureaucratic mind as we do, many military restrictions simply multiply unnecessary red tape rather than protect vital military secrets.

Thus, security investigations have been made of scientists engaged in open, basic research where there was no question of secret material being used; in these cases, the National Science Foundation has warned, "loyalty or security-type investigations are clearly undesirable and unlikely to serve any useful purpose."[4] "Security" regulations have suppressed medical research devoted entirely to such non-military problems as high blood pressure and multiple sclerosis. Dr. Fritz Zwicky, eminent professor of astrophysics at California Institute of Technology, was suspended from guided missile work simply because he chose to retain his Swiss citizenship. Such absurd procedures should be altered.[5] Professor Alfred Bornemann has written:

---

[4]National Science Foundation, Fifth Annual Report, 1955.

[5]See Walter Gellhorn, *Individual Freedom and Governmental Restraints* (Baton Rouge: L.S.U.

> whether or not a policy of secrecy was ever justified, in the past, it can scarcely be justified for security reasons and longer. ... Freedom of thought and enterprise is essential. ... Military success itself has always depended in the past on the effects or products of free thought and private enterprise in inter-war periods.

And Professor Arnold Zurcher has warned that a policy of governmental secrecy threatens to render ineffectual the very basis of democracy: an informed public opinion.[6]

What, then, should the government do about the nation's supply of scientists? We have seen that a program of positive intervention

---

Press, 1956), pp. 42–43, 168–68; *Medical Research: A Mid-century Survey* (Boston: Little Brown, 1955), vol. 1, pp. 185–89; John T. Edsall, "Government and the Freedom of Science," *Science* 121 (1955): 615.

[6]Alfred Bornemann, "Atomic Energy and Enterprise Economics," *Land Economics* (August, 1954): 202; Arnold J. Zurcher, "Democracy's Declining Capacity to Govern," *Western Political Quarterly* (December, 1955): 536–37. Also see Arthur A. Ekirch, Jr., *The Civilian and the Military* (New York: Oxford University Press, 1956), p. 276.

in the free market—such as been true of the Federal aid to over one-fourth of the nation's graduate science students, amounting to $26 million in 1954—only distorts the allocations of the free enterprise economy, and can only prove self-defeating. We have seen that any shortage that does occur is cured most rapidly and effectively by the rise in salaries for these scarce jobs that occurs swiftly if undramatically on the free market. And we have seen that the best that government can do to sure any shortage of military scientists, is to be willing to pay, or see its private contractors pay, salaries at their free market worth, and to remove unnecessary restrictions and red tape on scientific activity. In short: the government does its best and most constructive job, not by positive intervention into the society, but by repealing its own restrictions on free activity, by lifting its own burdens from the scientific, or indeed any other, sector of society.

If government can cure a shortage of military scientists by these means, should it do anything at all to encourage a general increase of scientists, military and civilian? We have seen that it can only defeat its own purposes, and distort the economy, by positive intervention.

But it can do other useful things to encourage science: acts that are not intervention, but are a repealing and loosening of its own policies that have been hampering the supply of scientists.

Thus, in the critical field of education, which is the ultimate source of scientists, the government can remove its own repressions on science education. For example, the entire philosophy of public education in this country needs an overhauling. This has been recently pointed out in ever-growing force, in quarters ranging from Admiral Rickover to *Life Magazine*. In short, we must abandon the mind-crippling "life adjustment" philosophy of our schools, which rather indoctrinates children in "group adjustment" than equips them with the mental skills and disciplines of science or any other intellectual subject. Our schools must once again regard it as their basic function to teach subjects, to encourage the rapid maturation of bright young minds. The present educational structure drags all the students down to the level of the lowest common denominator, passes all students, teaches rubbish rather than subject disciplines, and allows hooligans to widen their "self-expression" by tormenting and distracting those eager to learn—all in the name of "democracy." We shall never know how many potentially bright youngsters who could have been able and even great scientists, have been permanently crippled by the "progressive" education philosophy dominant in the public schools. (The Russians, be it said, abandoned the absurdities of "progressive" education many years ago, and to that extent enjoy superior scientific training.) The public schools are the responsibilities of the state governments, and therefore it is up to the states to transform their schools into "halls of learning."[7]

There are importance corollaries to this task of the states in reforming their own public schools. There is the problem of the uneducable youth—those too dumb or too uninterested to benefit from formal schooling, and who would be much happier at a job

---

[7]Typical of the recently growing mass of literature on this subject are Admiral Hyman Rickover, *Education and Freedom*, Arthur Bestor, *Restoration of Learning and Educational Wastelands*, Augustin Rudd, *Bending the Twig*, and publications of the Council of Basic Education, and many others.

or trade. The states should consider reducing the maximum age of compulsory attendance, or even repealing the compulsory attendance law altogether. Another important problem is the recent hullabaloo about teachers' salaries. Roger Freeman has conclusively shown, in a definite study, that there is no teachers' shortage whatever, present or future.[8] Freeman shows that teachers' salaries are fully adequate. There is, to be sure, a shortage of high-quality teachers, who are driven out of the profession by the absolutely uniform payscales, insisted upon by the teachers' unions. Robbed of incentives for merit, and frustrated by the red-tape of bureaucracy and civil service and by the absurdities of progressive education, the good teachers—the very ones who are needed to educate the young properly—leave for the better salaries they can obtain elsewhere. This is particularly true for the good science teachers—for industry and government have more job opportunities for ex-science teachers than for other teachers. The

[8]See Roger A. Freeman, *School Needs in the Decade Ahead* (Washington, D.C.: The Institute for Social Science Research, 1958).

public schools, therefore, should (1) pay good teachers more than poor ones; and (2) should pay science teachers more than others, so as not to lose them to other jobs. In short, not overall salaries, but the salary differentials, need overhauling—by officials who must have the courage to battle the entrenched bureaucracy of the NEA and other teachers' unions. While this is a state and local responsibility, the Federal government should certainly lend more encouragement to the states in this needed reform.

Another important state policy would be to relax the absurd regulations which states now require for hiring school teachers. These rules play into the hand of the professional progressive educationists by requiring a myriad of "method" courses before a man can teach in the schools, in the meanwhile slighting the all-important subject matter. Our greatest physicists are legally debarred from teaching in the public schools because they lack the "qualifications" imposed by state laws. Here, too, the states restrict the supply of teachers, especially the able ones who wish to stress knowledge of subject over progressive methodology.

To sum up, the proper role of government is to confine itself to removing the shackles that it has imposed on the supply and training of scientists. The Federal government could: stop paying lower than free-market salaries to scientists doing military work, and eliminate needless restrictions on the freedom of scientists; the state and local governments could overhaul the public school system by: transforming progressive into real education; relaxing or eliminating compulsory attendance laws; replacing uniform teachers' pay by merit differentials, and relatively higher salaries for science teachers; and eliminating the restrictions on the supply of teachers not indoctrinated with educationist methodology.

4. Specific Problems: The Alleged Scarcity of Scientific Research

In addition to complaints of a shortage of scientists, charges abound that scientific research, left to the mercies of the free market, would be insufficient for modern technological needs. The general principles of government policy in this field we have already set forth: (a) leaving the general allocation of resources purely to the free market—the profit and loss incentive and test of the free market being the only efficient way of allocating a country's resources in the way best calculated to satisfy consumer demand. This principle applies fully as well to scientific research as to any other sphere; and (b) for the military needs of research, acting only as a consumer rather than as a producer using funds to pay for private scientific contractors. In actual practice, the Federal government is already doing a great deal (although, as we shall see below, it can do much more) in this direction, by channeling most of its military research funds into private contractors, whom the military sees to be more efficient than government operation.[9]

Let us first turn to the problem of general research, however. Is it really true that such research will be deficient on the free market?

We have, first, been hearing a great deal of how much resources the Soviet Union has been putting into scientific research, and how we must redouble our efforts in order to catch up. But the National Science Foundation has estimated that the Soviet Union has been putting a little over 1 percent of its

---

[9]In 1953–54, the Federal government spent $2.81 billion of its funds on scientific research and development; of this amount, only $970 million was spent on programs within the government itself (and most of this was development rather than research); the remainder was channeled into private hands to pay for privately-conducted research ($1.5 billion in industry, $280 million in colleges).

national product into research and development. The Steelman Report of 1947 called for the United States to place 1 percent of its national product into research and development, in the years ahead. Yet, we now have 2 percent of our product going into "R and D," and our national income is far, far higher than that of the Soviets.[10] In 1953–54, private sources contributed $2.6 billion to R and D; this contrasts to a total of $530 million of private funds in 1941. In fact, with the exception of pure, or basic, research (which we will study further below) the National Science Foundation's study conceded the sufficiency of private scientific research in American industry.

The flourishing of private research in our modern age has been eloquently hailed by General David Sarnoff, board chairman of RCA:

> Today, science and industry are linked by arteries of progress and their lifeblood

[10]See *Basic Research, A National Resource* (Washington, D.C.: National Science Foundation, 1957); and John Steelman, *Science and Public Policy* (Washington, D.C., 1947).

> is technical research. ... The pattern of our industrial progress ... lies in a partnership between those who create good things and those who produce and distribute and service them. It lies in teamwork between research and industry.[11]

We have seen that government subsidization or operation of non-military research would distort the efficient allocation of resources of the free market economy. It would do more; as Sarnoff pointed out, government aid would inevitably mean "increased government control of the daily lives of all the people." Secondly, government control would tragically bureaucratize science and cripple that spirit of free inquiry on which all scientific advance must rest:

> government control of research would destroy the very qualities that enable researchers to make such an important contribution to society. For government control means that rigid lines would be

[11]Brig. Gen. David Sarnoff, *Research and Industry: Partners in Progress* (Address, Nov. 14, 1951), pp. 6–7.

> set for research; and these lines may not meet changing requirements. Certainly industry is best qualified to define its own research needs. And the partnership between research and industry loses its meaning when government can dictate the subject and objective of research in any competitive system of private enterprise.[12]

The myth has arisen that government research is made necessary by our technological age, because only planned, directed, large-scale "team" research can produce important inventions or develop them properly. The day of the individual or small-scale inventor is supposedly over and done with. And the strong inference is that government, as potentially the "largest-scale" operator, must play a leading role in even non-military scientific research. This common myth has been completely exploded by the researches of John Jewkes, David Sawers, and Richard Stillerman in their highly important

[12]Sarnoff, *Research and Industry*, pp. 12 ff.

recent work.[13,14] Taking sixty-one of the most important inventions of the twentieth century (excluding atomic energy, which we will discuss below), Jewkes et al. found that more than half of these were the work of individual inventors—with the individuals working at their own directions, and with very limited resources. In this category they place such inventions as: air-conditioning, automatic transmission, bakelite, the ballpoint pen, catalytic cracking of petroleum, cellophane, the cotton picker, the cyclotron, gas refrigeration, the electron microscope, the gyro-compass, the helicopter, insulin, the jet engine, Kodachrome, magnetic recording, penicillin, the Polaroid camera, radio, the safety razor, titanium, and the zipper. The jet

---

[13]John Jewkes, David Sawers, and Richard Stillerman, *The Sources of Invention* (New York: St. Martin's Press, 1958).

[14]Typical recent expressions of the myth may be found in John Kenneth Galbraith, *American Capitalism*; W. Rupert Maclaurin, "The Sequence from Invention to Innovation," *Quarterly Journal of Economics* (February 1953); Waldemar B. Kaempffert, *Invention and Society* (1930); A. Coblenz and H.L. Owens, *Transistors: Theory and Application* (New York: McGraw Hill, 1955).

engine was invented and carried through its early development, practically simultaneously, by Britons and Germans who were individual inventors, either completely unconnected with the aircraft industry or not specialists in engines. The gyro-compass was invented by a young German art historian. The bulk of the basic inventions for radio came from individual inventors unconnected with communications firms, some of whom created new small firms of their own to exploit the invention. The cyclotron was invented and partly developed by a university scientist, using simple equipment in the early stages. Penicillin was invented and partly developed in a university laboratory, and insulin was invented by a general practitioner who used a university laboratory.

Of the inventions studied that were achieved in industrial research laboratories, some arose in small firms, others were more or less accidental by-products of other work rather than preplanned and predirected. Terylene, the synthetic fiber, was discovered by a small research group in a firm not directly interested in fiber production. The process of continuous hot strip rolling of steel sheets was thought up by an individual inventor and then perfected in a small steel company. The LP record was invented by an engineer working on it as an individual sideline, and then was developed by another corporation.

In other cases, inventions in the research laboratories of large companies were made by small research teams, often centered around one outstanding man. Such was the case with Nylon, at the DuPont laboratories.[15]

The twentieth century has produced some great independent inventors, creators of many important new devises. One of them, the Englishman S.G. Brown (components for telegraphy, telephony, radio, and gyro-compass) declared: "if there were any control over me or my work every idea would stop." Brown never accepted financial aid for experimental

[15]For other experts who believe that a highly important role still remains for the individual independent inventor, see Joseph Rossman, *The Psychology of the Inventor*; the late Charles F. Kettering, *New York Times*, March 12, 1950; W.J. Kroll (the inventor of ductile titanium), "How Commercial Titanium and Zirconium Were Born," *Journal of the Franklin Institute* (September 1955); and H.S. Hatfield, *The Inventor and His World* (West Drayton, U.K.: Penguin, 1948).

work, or for producing a new device. How would such a man fare under the control of a government-directed research team, or one that was government-controlled? P.T. Farnsworth, great television pioneer, has always preferred to do his research on a small scale and with simple equipment. F.W. Lanchester, great British inventor in aerodynamics and engineering once wrote:

> the salient feature of my career ... (is that) ... my work has been almost wholly individual. My scientific and technical work has been almost wholly individual. My scientific and technical work has never been backed by funds from external sources to any material extent.

Lee de Forest, eminent inventor of the radio vacuum tube, always found it difficult to work under any conditions short of complete autonomy. Sir Frank Whittle invented the jet engine with very slim resources.

C.F. Kettering often positively preferred simple equipment. And R.M. Lodge recently warned:

> The trend towards more and more complex apparatus should be carefully watched and controlled; otherwise the

> scientists themselves gradually become specialist machine-minders, and there is a tendency, for example, for an analytical problem to be passed from the micro-analytical laboratory to the infra-red laboratory and from there to the mass spectrographic laboratory, whereas all the time all that was needed was a microphone and a keen observer.[16]

The worthy individual inventor is far from helpless in the modern world. He may, in a free enterprise system, become a free-lance consultant to industry, may work on inventions on outside grants, may sell his ideas to corporations, may form or be backed by a research association (both profit and non-profit), or may obtain aid from special private organizations that invest risk capital in small speculative inventions (e.g., the American Research and Development Corporations).

---

[16]R.M. Lodge, *Economic Factors in Planning of Research*, 1954. Quoted in Jewkes, et al., *Sources of Invention*, p. 133. On other cases of great scientists preferring simple equipment, see: John Randal Baker, *The Scientific Life* (1942); P. Freedman, *The Principles of Scientific Research*; J.B.S. Haldane, *Science Advances* (New York: Macmillan, 1947).

One very important reason for the success of the independent inventor, and his preservation from the dominance of large-scale government-controlled projects, stem from the very nature of invention: "The essential feature of innovation is that the path to it is not known beforehand. The less, therefore, an inventor is pre-committed in his speculation by training or tradition, the better the chance of his escaping from the grooves of accepted thought."[17] There are many recorded instances of the inventor winning out despite the scoffing of the recognized experts in the field, perhaps even emboldened because he didn't know enough to be discouraged. One authority maintains that Farnsworth benefited from his lack of contact with the outside scientific world. Once, a professor gave him four good reasons why his idea—later successful—could not possibility work. Before the discovery of the transistor, many scientists claimed that nothing more could be learned in that field. Eminent mathematicians once claimed to prove logically that short-wave radio was impossible. Government-controlled research

[17]Jewkes, et al., *Sources of Invention*, p. 116.

would undoubtedly rely on existing authorities, and thus would snuff out the searching of the truly original minds. Many of the great inventors of recent times could not have gotten a research job in the field for lack of expertise: the inventors of Kodachrome were musicians; Eastman, the great inventor in photography, was a bookkeeper at the time; the inventor of the ball-point pen was an artist and journalist; the automatic dialing system was invented by an undertaker; a veterinarian invented the pneumatic tire. Furthermore, there are many inventors who are part-time, or one-shot, inventors, who are clearly more useful on their own than as part of a research team.

As the eminent British zoologist John Baker points out, the life of an independent researcher involves the willingness to bear great risks: "The life is too strenuous for most people, and the timid scientist hankers after the safety of directed teamwork routine. The genuine research worker is altogether different kind of person."[18] Darwin once wrote: "I am like a gambler and love a wild experiment."

[18]John Randal Baker, *Science and the Planned State* (New York: Macmillan Co., 1945), p. 42.

The importance of self-directed work to great scientists is stressed by the Nobel prize-winning chemical discoverer of vitamins, Szent-Gyorgyi, who wrote:

> The real scientist ... is ready to bear privation ... rather than let anyone dictate to him which direction his work must take.[19]

Not only inventors, but many types of scientists benefit from the work of independent researchers in their fields. Einstein said that: "I am a horse for single harness, not cut out for team work," and suggested that refugee scientists take jobs as lighthouse-keepers, so that they could enjoy needed isolation. The fundamental discoveries in valence theory, cytogenetics, embryology, and many other fields of twentieth-century biology, were made by individual scientists.[20] Scientific discoveries, furthermore, cannot be planned in advance.

---

[19]A. Szent-Gyorgyi, "Science Needs Freedom," *World Digest* 55 (1943): 50.

[20]See Baker, *Science and the Planned State*, pp. 49–52. Baker comments on the lack of originality of research teams, who tend to be better at following up the leads of others than at originating ideas themselves.

They grow out of apparently unrelated efforts of previous scientists, often in diverse fields. The radium and X-ray treatments for cancer owe most, not to planned research on cancer cures, but to the discoverers of radium and X-rays, who were working for quite different goals. Baker shows that the discovery of a treatment for cancer of the prostate emerged out of centuries of unrelated research on: the prostate, phosphatase, and on hormones, none of which was aimed toward a cancer cure.[21]

---

[21] Ibid., pp. 59–60:

> Our modern knowledge of how to control cancer of the prostate is due to the researches of these men—of Hunter, Gruber, Griffiths, Steinach, and Kun on the prostate; of Grosses, Rusler, Davis, Baaman, and Riedell on phosphatase; and of Kutcher and Wolbergs on phosphatase in the prostate. Not one of these men was studying cancer, yet without them, the discovery of the new treatment could not have been made. What central planner, interested in the cure of cancer, would have supported Griffiths in his studies on the seasonal cycle of the

Apart from individual scientists and inventors, there is also great need for the existence of small research laboratories in small firms as well as in large ones. There is an inevitable clash between practical administrators of research and the scientists themselves, and the evils of bureaucratic administration and crippling of scientific endeavor will be infinitely greater if science is under the control of direction of the Ultimate Bureaucracy of government.[22]

---

hedgehog, or Grosser and Husler in their biochemical work on the lining membrane of the intestine? How could anyone have connected phosphatase with cancer, when the existence of phosphatase was unknown? And while it was yet unknown, how could the man in charge of the cancer funds know to whom to give the money for research? No planner could make the right guesses.

[22]On the inevitable clash between research administrators and scientists, see: Jewkes, et al., *Sources of Invention*, pp. 132ff.; K. Ziegler, *The Indivisibility of Research* (1955); S.C. Harland, "Recent Progress in the Breeding of Cotton for Quality," *Journal of the Textile Institute* (Great Britain) (February 1955);

O.E. Buckley, when president of the Bell Telephone Laboratories, stated: "one sure way to defeat the scientific spirit is to attempt to direct enquiry from above. All successful industrial research directors know this and have learnt by experience that one thing a director of research must never do is to direct research." Similar views have been expressed by C.E.K. Mees, of Eastman Kodak, and Sir Alexander Fleming, discoverer of penicillin, who said:

> certain industrial places ... put up a certain amount of money for research and hire a team. They often direct them on the particular problems they are going to work out. This is a very good way of employing a certain number of people, paying salaries, and not getting very much in return.[23]

Jewkes and his colleagues, describing the best ways of crippling a research organization,

---

R.N. Anthony, *Management Controls in Industrial Research Organization* (Graduate School of Business Administration, Harvard University, 1953).

[23]From L.J. Ludovivi, "Fleming, Discoverer of Penicillin," cited in Jewkes, et al., *Sources of Invention.*

might have had a typical government operation or control in mind:

> The chances of success are further reduced where the research group is organized in hierarchical fashion, with ideas and instructions flowing downwards and not upwards ... where the direction to research is ... closely defined ... where men are asked to report at regular intervals ... where achievements are constantly being recorded and assessed; where spurious cooperation is enforced by time-wasting committees and paper work.[24]

In gauging the effectiveness of large vs. small-scale research, we should remember that whether or not a firm engages in research at all (apart from government contract) depends on the type of industry it is in. The great bulk of manufacturing firms, for example, do not engage in research and development at all The one-tenth that do, are mostly in technologically advanced and advancing industries, where expanding scientific knowledge is needed, and where many scien-

[24]Jewkes, et al., *Sources of Invention*, pp. 141–42.

tists must be hired anyway for test and control work. On the other hand, industries that rely more on empirical rather than scientific knowledge do less research. Some large-scale industries, like chemicals, do a great deal of research; while others, such as iron and steel, do much less. Some small-scale industries do little research, while others, like scientific instrument firms, do a relatively great amount. And while the bulk of industrial research is done by the very large firms, we have seen the vital role of the independent inventor (and later we shall see further the crucial role of the university laboratory in basic research). Furthermore, it has been found that in those firms that do conduct research, the number of research workers per 100 employees is higher for the small, and lowest for the large firms.[25]

It should be noted that few of the Nobel Prize winners since 1900 came from the

[25]This is borne out in separate studies by the U.S. Department of Labor, *Scientific Research and Development in American Industry*, Bulletin #1148, Washington, 1953; and the National Association of Manufacturers, *Trends in Industrial Research and Patent Practices.*

large industrial research laboratories. Furthermore, many of the current research labs of the big corporations originated as small firms, which were later bought by the big corporation. This happened with General Motors, and with General Electric. The large corporations also make a great deal of use of outside consultants and independent research organizations (both profit and non-profit making). This certainly must confound the partisan of organized, large-scale government-controlled and directed research: for if organized, large-scale research is invariably more efficient, why do these big corporations bother with small outside firms? Here are some of the reasons given by the big firms themselves:

> They may be short of trained people. Or they may be confronted with a task of a non-continuing nature which they prefer to have out to others ... or they may be confronted with a type of technical problem new to them which they feel they cannot handle at all. Or, having been continually defeated by some technical problem, they may hand out the

> task to others who will come to it with fresh minds and no preconceptions.[26]

Resistance of an organization to new ideas has occurred significantly even in efficient, alert corporations—how much more would it occur in government, where there is neither the incentive nor the possibility of a profit-and-loss check on its efficiency! Thus: the telephone, cable, and electric manufacturing companies were originally apathetic about the possibilities of wireless telegraphy; RCA resisted Armstrong's FM ideas; the Edison Company, at the turn of the century, scoffed at the idea of a gas motor for transportation, insisting on the future of the electric motor for that purpose; the established aircraft-engine firms scoffed at the jet engine and at the retractable under-carriage; the British and American chemical firms were highly critical of penicillin, and almost refused to take part in its development; The Marconi Company expressed no interest in television when it was brought to their attention in 1925; the manufacturers of navigational equipment took no part in the invention of the gyro-compass.

---

[26]Jewkes, et al., *Sources of Invention*, pp. 188–89.

When the Ford Motor Company sought to introduce automation in their factories, they turned to the small specialized firms in the machine-tool industry, "The small uninhibited firms with no preconceived notions." And even Henry Ford resisted the thermostat, or hydraulic brakes.

Furthermore, in many of our biggest industries, the critical innovations of the twentieth century have come from outside the big firms. Of the three big inventions in the aluminum industry up to 1937, two came from men outside the industry—despite the fact that ALCOA had an aluminum monopoly during those years. The two significant new ideas in steel-making in this century came from a newcomer and from one of the smaller steel firms (continuous hot strip rolling), and the other from an individual German inventor (continuous casting). The large-scale, progressive automotive industry has benefited a great deal from outside ideas—including automatic transmissions and power steering, and small firms and accessory manufacturers have contributed new systems of suspension. In the progressive, large-scale petroleum industry, which devotes heavy expenditures to research, many leading ideas have come from small firms or outside individuals including catalytic cracking: "Looking back dispassionately we find that (the major oil companies) mainly took up and developed ideas, which were brought to them by men who did not, in the first instance, belong to their own team."[27]

Another important point is that most industrial research laboratories, even in the large companies, are themselves small; more than one-half of the laboratories in the U.S. employ less than 15 scientists, and most of these are for routine or development work, rather than research. The average operating cost of a laboratory per research scientists is about $25,000—not a prohibitive sum for an average sized firm. Moreover, 49 percent of all firms holding patents, in 1953, had fewer than 5,000 employees all told.

Many laboratories, while remaining at the same size, have fluctuated greatly in their failure or success over time, depending on the qualities of their personnel and, above all,

---

[27]P.H. Frankel, *Essentials of Petroleum*, 1946, p. 148. Quoted in Jewkes, et al., *Sources of Invention*.

their leadership. The leading inventors in these laboratories themselves stress the virtues of small groups. Fermi has said: "Efficiency does not increase proportionately with numbers. A large group creates complicated administrative problems, and much effort is spent on organization." And, in a striking anticipation of Parkinson's Law of Bureaucracy, S.C. Harland wrote this about the large lab:

> You see crowds of people milling around with an air of fictitious activity, behind a façade of massive mediocrity. There is a kind of Malthusianism acting on research institutes. Just as a population will breed up to the available food supply, research institutes will enlarge themselves as long as the money holds out.[28]

We may proceed now from research proper to the field of development. It has been argued that, while small scale basic research may continue to be important, the cost of developing already-created inventions is growing

---

[28]Harland, *Recent Progress in the Breeding of Cotton for Quality*. Also see Laura Fermi, "Atoms in the Family," p. 185. Quoted in Jewkes, et al., *Sources of Invention*, p. 162.

ever-greater, and is therefore peculiarly susceptible of large-scale organized and directed effort. Most of the technological work in the industrial laboratories, indeed, is the actual development of new methods and products, while university and other educational laboratories have relatively concentrated on pure research.

Development costs have grown more expensive especially in the chemical industries, where a new idea is taken and run through very large-scale empirical experimentation (e.g., the trial-and-error searching for a better strain of penicillin among a large number of possible molds). Increased caution in developing products, greater testing for quality and safety, a heavy initial advertising campaign to introduce new products—all these factors have increased the costs of development in modern times (although, with technological advance cheapening everything else, we may expect it to lower costs of development as well).

But a crucial point about development has been often overlooked: how much of resources to put into development as against other things, how fast to develop at any given time, is a risky decision on the part of a firm. The decision depends upon the firm's estimates of future costs, sales, profits, etc. Government, crippling or eliminating the free market signals of prices and costs, would be lost without a guide to efficiency or allocation of resources. Further, the main reason a firm decides to devote its resources in an attempt at speedy development is the spur of competition. And competition means the free, unhampered market. Even in the case of Nylon, the most cited example on behalf of large-scale monopoly research and development, DuPont had the competitive spur of knowing that German scientists were also working on similar synthetic fibers.

Where the competitive spur is weak, or especially non-existent (as in government), development will be slowed down. Furthermore, the existence of many firms, many centers of development, make it far more likely that new ideas will obtain a hearing and a trial somewhere. General Electric, when dominant in lighting, was sluggish in developing fluorescent lighting, but once other firms entered the field, it sprang to life and regained a dominant position through its new-found efficiency. As Jewkes and his associates sum up:

> Against the claim that the prerogative in development should always rest with the biggest and the most securely established industrial organizations, may be set, therefore, the advantages of the attack from many angles. The tasks of development are themselves of such diversity and of so varying a scale that it may be a ... dangerous oversimplification to suppose that they can always be best handled by any single type of institution.[29]

The best condition, they add, is a variety of firms, in size and in outlook—some bold and other cautious, some leading and others following.

Even in the field of development proper, in fact, many important new products have come from small-sized firms, or even individuals. These include: air conditioning, automatic transmissions, bakelite, cellophane tape, magnetic recording, quick freezing,

---

[29]Jewkes, et al., *Sources of Invention*, p. 222.

power steering, crease-resistant textiles, and ram-jet aircraft.

Professor Baker has preferred another important refutation of the statist claim that governmental monopoly direction of research would eliminate "wasteful overlapping" of effort. Baker points to the enormous importance for scientists, in having two or more mutually independent scientists or laboratories confirming each other's conclusions. Only then can the world of science consider the experiment truly confirmed.[30]

---

[30]Baker, *Science and the Planned State*, p. 49:

> There is one occurrence ... which helps the scientist form a valid judgment better than anything else. This is the ... publication of the same result by two entirely independent workers. Central planners are inclined to consider that one of the two independent workers has been wasting his time. The actual research worker knows that this is not so. It is the very fact that the two workers are independent that inclines others to accept their findings. Scarcely a working scientist will deny that two independent papers containing the same result are very much

more convincing than a single paper by two collaborators ... (also) each paper has a different outlook, and the reading of the two papers is far more stimulating and suggestive.

5.
Soviet Science

"Planned" science sounds impressive; actually it means prohibited science, where no scientist can follow the leads of his own creative ideas. We have heard a great deal recently about the alleged glories of Soviet science, and about the necessity of the United States catching up with such wonders as sputniks. What is the real record of Soviet science? Professor Baker, analyzing this record, shows that, at the beginnings of the Soviet Union, the old pre-revolutionary scientists continued to do well, largely because science was not yet under government planning. That came with the Second Five-Year Plan, in 1932. The Plan set forth very broad subjects for investigation, but, by the nature of such a plan, many important areas were excluded from the required agenda.

> Take almost any branch of non-revolutionary biological science in which outstanding discoveries were made in the outside world during the years of the plan, and you are likely to find that the whole subject was excluded from study.[31]

For example; the study of hormones, and genetics. The Lysenko controversy, the use of the State to eradicate the science of genetics in Soviet Russia, and the compulsory twisting of truth by the Soviet State to fit the ideological myths of its rulers, are well-known, but can hardly be overstressed. It is important to realize that it is not simply because the Soviet or Nazi leaders were particularly perverse men that they reached out to prevent or cripple science's drive for truth; but because such actions are inherent in the very nature of statism, and central planning. Power, and its promotion, advancement of the ideology of power, become the highest social goal, before which all truth, all integrity must give way.

Government control of science, government planning of science, is bound to result in the politicization of science, the substitution

---

[31]Baker, *Science and the Planned State*, pp. 66 ff.

of political goals and political criteria for scientific ones. Even pro-Soviet scientists have admitted that Soviet research is inferior to American, that basic, as contrasted to applied, research, is neglected; that there is too much red tape; that little fundamentally creative work has been done; and that science is unduly governed by political considerations—such as the political views of the scientist propounding any given theory. Scientists are shot for taking the view that happens to be in political disfavor. And, as Baker concludes:

> If the selection of scientific personnel is left to the State, the wrong ones are likely to be given important posts, because those who are not themselves scientists will be led astray by ... false claims and pretences ... (and) scientists may exhibit a servile obedience to their political bosses.[32]

No wonder that in a list, drawn up by seven scientists, of the two dozen most important scientific discoveries made between World Wars I and II, not one came from the U.S.S.R.

[32]Ibid., pp. 75–76.

In a follow-up to his earlier book, Dr. Baker has recently reaffirmed these conclusions. He further describes the coerced eradication of genetic science in Russia. He also deprecates the much-touted sputniks.[33] In the first place, if one starts with a given end, and the knowledge of how to get there has already been attained, one can arrive at the end in proportion to the resources one is willing to throw into the undertaking—all this then becomes a purely engineering and economic problem, rather than a scientific research problem, where ends or means are not yet known.[34] If, for some military or propagandist purpose, it was desirable to make a very deep hole toward the center of the earth, the deepest holes would probably be made by whichever nation decided to devote the largest amount of money to the project. The same principle applies to the sputniks.[35] And, even

---

[33]John R. Baker, *Science and the Sputniks* (London: Society for Freedom in Science, December 1958). Also see Dr. Conway Zirkle, *Death of a Science in Russia* (Philadelphia, 1949).

[34]Baker, *Science and the Sputniks*, p. 1.

[35]Ibid.

so, Baker points out, American satellites have far superior instrumentation, and are therefore much more important scientifically.

6.
The Inefficiency of Military Research by Government

We have now seen that general scientific research should be left to the free market, and that conditions of modern technology do not require government control or planning of science. Quite the contrary. What now about military research? We have already said briefly that the end in view is for government to be only a consumer of military research rather than a producer; that government should contract for scientific research rather than conduct its own. Confirmation for this position comes from the important report of the Hoover Commission Task Force Report on Research Activities.[36] The report was made by scientists who were mainly advisers to the Department of Defense, and hence not sympathetic to the Department.

The Task Force found that three-fifths of the military funds spent by government in 1955 were on operations in private laboratories. All of the Defense Department's basic research was carried on in private laboratories—a clear admission that government laboratories are not good places to conduct vital basic research. Most of this basic research is done in college and university labs, its traditional home. The Task Force comments:

> Since there is, in general, an inadequate environment and competence for basic research in its (Dept. of Defense) laboratories, the placing of substantially all of this work in the laboratories of the civilian economy is necessary.[37]

---

[36]Subcommittee of the Commission on Organization of the Executive Branch of Government, *Research Activities in the Department of Defense and Defense-Related Agencies* (Washington. D.C.: April, 1955).

[37]Ibid., p. 36.

As for applied research, two-thirds was being done in the civilian contract labs, and the Task Force strongly recommended the shift of most of the remaining one-third to private civilian hands: "A large portion of the applied research done in the laboratories of the military could be done more effectively in those of the civilian economy." As for actual development of products, as compared to research, the Task Force also advocates a larger role for private operation. Development occurs in several steps. There is (a) establishment of the weapon project. This of course must be decided ultimately by the government staff, but here again, technical studies in connection with establishment are being farmed out to private contractors; (b) testing, which of course must be done by government—the consumer; (c) development and design. This category also absorbs two-thirds of all government R and D funds; three-fourths of development and design work was being done in private contract laboratories, and one-fourth in the government, and yet the Hoover Task Force declared: "Perhaps one-half of the work done in the laboratories of the military can readily be placed in the civilian economy."[38] (Other development activities are development aids to products, and current development, in which there is considerable activity by government.)

The overall assessment of the Task Force: "a considerable portion of the work now done in installations of the Government should be done in the civilian economy"—especially in applied research, and in development and design. This would be "placing the work where it can be performed with the greatest effectiveness." And the Task Force expressed concern with the fact that, in recent years, the percentage of R and D work done in the government has been slowly but steadily increasing.

What are the reasons given by the Hoover Task Force for this relative inefficiency of government military scientific research? One reason is the salary problem. We have seen above the "shortage" that comes from not paying the free market price for services. The Task Force found that the pay for civil service scientists in the Defense Department has

[38]Ibid., p. 38.

not been sufficient to meet the competition of the free market, and that there have been too few scientists appointed in the upper levels. Other problems are inherent in military operations in government. The system of military officer-rotation prohibits the emergence of a long-run specialized career for scientific officers. As the Task Forces charges:

> the high level of strength of the industrial research and development organization of the nation could not have been attained were the personnel policy for the professional staff the equivalent of that of the military services for their technical officers.[39]

Investigating three of the best Naval laboratories, the Task Force found an unfavorable "atmosphere" of friction among mixed civilian and military personnel, problems due to inadequate civil service pay and promotion policies, and to rapid rotation of upper officers. (And here we may emphasize the recommendation made above about scientists in government: that if the armed forces

---

[39]Ibid., p. 44.

want good scientists, they should pay market wages, remove undue restrictions, and, further, to change the civil service system to allow more merit payment and less fixed bureaucracy.)

But there is more to governmental inefficiency than those matters. The Hoover Task Force asked the question: why is government poor on all research and development and design, but relatively effective in such work as testing and establishment? Because, answers the Task Force,

> The operations of research and development are highly creative and imaginative, they require men with a special type of qualification and a high level of ... training. Most of the operations of the establishment, placement, and monitoring of programs, and the tests for evaluation are much less creative and more engineering in their nature.[40]

But even in these latter tasks, the Task Force adds, there is much room for improvement.

---

[40]Ibid., p. 48.

The Task Force found the Air Force with the best record in shunting scientific operations to the civilian private economy, and the Army the poorest. But it called for even the Air Force to do more to shift operations into private hands.

7.
Atomic Energy

We have so far omitted discussion of atomic energy. Our nuclear age has been held up as the chief argument of those who believe that government control and direction of science is necessary in the modern world—at the very least, in the atomic field. The government-directed team effort involved in making the atomic bomb has been glorified as the model to be imitated by science in the years ahead. But, in analyzing this common view, Jewkes, Sawers, and Stillerman point out, first, that the fundamental atomic discoveries had been made by academic scientists working with simple equipment. One of the greatest of these scientists has commented: "we could not afford elaborate equipment, so we had to think."[41]

Furthermore, virtually the entire early work on atomic energy, up to the end of 1940, was financed by private foundations and universities.[42] And the development of the bomb was, for peacetime purposes, an extremely wasteful process. The friction on the project between scientists and administrators, the great difficulties of administration, has been pointed out often.[43] Moreover, Jewkes, Sawers, and Stillerman suggest that government control of research slowed down, rather than speeded up, peacetime atomic development—especially with its excessive secrecy and restrictions. They warn also that latest estimates hold that, even by the year 2000, less than one-half of the total output of electricity will come from atomic energy (the main peacetime use), and that over-optimism about atomic energy has already drained scientists and technologists away from other fields, diminishing the supply of

---

[41]Jewkes, et al., *Sources of Invention*, p. 76.

[42]See Compton, *Atomic Quest*, p. 28.

[43]Ibid., p. 113.

research needed elsewhere. And Professor Bornemann warns that

> pressure of exploitation for military purposes has depleted the stock of basic scientific knowledge and in an atmosphere, moreover, which has not been conducive to further discovery in this realm.[44]

The eminent economic historian John Nef points out that such inventions useful to war as nitroglycerin and dynamite, did not emerge from war, but from developments in the mining industry. Nef finds that recent world wars have not so much stimulated scientific development, as diverted it into purely military tasks—in fact, have slowed down genuine scientific progress. And while the vast sums of the government speeded up the development of the bomb, "it cannot be claimed that war made the general use of this force for the material benefit of humanity more imminent." And a

---

[44]Bornemann, "Atomic Energy and Enterprise Economics," p. 196. Also see Department of State, Pub. #2702, *The International Control of Atomic Energy* (Washington, D.C.: Chemists' Association), *Impact of Peaceful Uses of Atomic Energy on the Chemical Industry* (Washington, D.C.: Feb. 1956).

prominent American engineer has noted that the armed forces, between the wars, were technologically stagnant, and that

> little technological progress is possible during a war, except of the 'hothouse' variety, which is forced and superficial, and that whatever gains have been made in military technology have come as a consequence of more general scientific and industrial advances.[45]

Bornemann charged further that government monopoly of the atom, and its lack of profit and loss incentives, made atomic power inefficient and over-costly. Government secrecy greatly delayed engineers of the power industry from learning about the modern technology, therefore slowing scientific development.

As we saw earlier, neither is Dr. John R. Baker impressed with such Soviet achievements as the sputnik as a model for science. Engineering development toward a specific given end—in addition to the other evils of

[45]John U. Nef, *War and Human Progress* (Cambridge: Harvard University Press, 1950), pp. 375–77, 448.

government control—also deprives basic research of needed scientific resources.[46]

That modern nuclear science has not rendered obsolete an individual inventor, the free and undirected spirit (see the views of Jewkes et al. discussed above) has recently been shown in dramatic form in the case of the "crazy Greek," Nicholas Christofilos, who, as an elevator engineer and supervisor for a truck repair depot, taught himself nuclear physics from the ground up, and originated theories so challenging that atomic experts scoffed and ignored him—until they proved successful. Christofilos, Dr. Edward Teller, and others have all indicated that, in his case, lack of training was a positive advantage in preserving his original bent of mind.[47]

If, then, the advent of atomic energy does not change our basic conclusions: that all civilian research and development be done by the free market, and that as much military scientific work as possible be channeled into private rather than government operations,

---

[46]See Baker, *Science and the Sputniks.*

[47]William Trombley, "Triumph is Space for a 'Crazy Greek,'" *Life* (March 30, 1959): 31–34.

what of the space age? How shall we finance our future explorations in space? The answer is simple: insofar as space explorations are a byproduct of needed military work (such as guided missiles) and only insofar, let the space exploration proceed on the same basis as any other military research. But, to the extent that it is not needed by the military, and is simply a romantic penchant for space exploration, then this penchant must take its chances, like everything, in the free market. It may seem exciting to engage in space exploration, but it is also enormously expensive, and wasteful of resources that could go into needed products to advance life on this earth. To the extent that voluntary funds are used in such endeavors, all well and good; but to tax private funds to engage in such ventures would be just another giant government boondoggle.[48]

Turning from the general to the particular, we find that in recent years the Federal government has begun to realize the superior efficiency of private enterprise, even in

[48]See Frank S. Meyer, "Principles and Heresies," *National Review* (November 8, 1958): 307.

atomic development. The Hoover Task Force found that the Atomic Energy Commission's nuclear plants were all operated as contract installations, by private industry or by universities. In 1954, the Atomic Energy Commission awarded nearly 18,000 prime contracts to over 5,000 firms, who in turn let more than 375,000 subcontracts. As a result, all the major productive facilities of the atomic energy program have been designed, built, equipped, and operated by private firms.[49] Furthermore, the Atomic Energy Act of 1954 significantly relaxed the Federal atomic monopoly, permitting much more private participation in atomic development. As soon as the Act was passed, private industry began moving successfully into the atomic field. Consolidated Edison announced plans for building a 200,000 kilowatt atomic power generating plant at Indian Point, New York—with no help whatever from government except permitting the company to buy atomic fuel. Other companies interested in getting into various phases

---

[49]See Council for Technological Advancement, *Industrial Participation in Atomic Energy Development* (October 18, 1954).

of an atomic power industry are: electric equipment manufacturers, and companies in other industries (e.g., aircraft, locomotives, machine tools, petroleum, etc.) looking for channels of diversification, and universities, medical and other research organizations, hoping to buy small atomic reactors.

Much, however, remains to be done, and existing restrictions and regulations still keep a large segment of industry from furthering atomic progress. The Atomic Energy Committee of Manufacturing Chemists' Association urge further liberalizing of security and patent regulations.[50] The AEC's powers of licensing and further regulating should be eliminated. The Atomic Energy Commission should confine its activities to military atomic energy; by subsidizing and regulating peaceful atomic energy; by subsidizing and regulating peaceful atomic power, it distorts market allocation of resources and prevents efficient operations. Federal subsidies to atomic power plants burden competing power plants from competing energy sources, and foster uneconomic use of resources.

[50] *Impact of Peaceful Uses* ..., p. 10.

Another important way in which the government could encourage peaceful atomic development in a manner consistent with the free market: by freeing it from governmental burdens, to eliminate rate regulation of public utilities (a job for the state governments). Public utilities are main potential users of atomic energy, but they could hardly do the job of which they are capable with their rates, and methods of operation, fixed by government authority. And the Federal government could properly stimulate space exploration, in a manner consistent with the free market, by permitting any private firms or organizations that might land on other planets, to own the land and other resources which they begin to exploit: in the manner of the Homestead law, although without the law's restrictions on acreage or use of land. Automatic government ownership of any new lands in space acts as an enormous damper on private exploration and development.

There has been much pressure, in recent years, by the firms about to enter the atomic energy industry (specifically the builders of atomic reactors), for Federal subsidies to supplement the third-party liability insurance available from private insurance companies: in cases where accidents at atomic plants injure third parties.[51] This pressure should be firmly resisted. If private enterprise, using its own funds, is unable to pay the full costs of its own insurance, then it should not enter the business. The promotion of atomic energy for peaceful uses is not an absolute goal, as we have seen; it must compete in use of resources with other power plants and with other industries. Any government subsidization of an enterprise, whether through insurance grants or any other method, weakens the private enterprise system and its basic principle that every firm must stand on its own voluntarily-raised resources, and distorts the efficient allocation of resources to serve consumer wants. The other enterprises in this country must pay for their own full insurance costs, and so should the atomic industry. The wise words of the Hoover Task Force on Lending Agencies should be heeded here:

---

[51]Thus see Paul F. Genachte, *Moving Ahead With the Atom* (New York: Chase Manhattan Bank, January 1957), p. 12.

> The risks of ownership are inseparably woven into the concept of private property. When an owner is relieved of his normal risks other than by his own effort and industry, he is beholden to those who assume the risks in his place. This increases the likelihood that he also will be relieved of the other attributes of property ownership—the right, for example, to decide how, when, where, and by whom the property shall be used. In the end he is likely to be relived of the property as well.[52]

[52]Task Force Report, Commission on Organization of the Executive Branch of the Government, Lending Agencies (Washington, D.C.: February, 1955), p. 9.

8.
BASIC RESEARCH

THE NATIONAL SCIENCE FOUNDATION, in its 1957 study of American research and development, concluded that "our overall effort is ample."[53] It also concluded, however, that we are deficient in basic research, and that this phase of R&D needs encouragement. It recommends a program of Federal encouragement, ranging from tax exemptions (see below) to Federal aid. We have seen, however, that the great bulk of basic research takes place in private university laboratories, and that the Hoover Task Force has found the government incompetent to perform even military research and development, much

[53]See *Basic Research, A National Resource.*

less civilian. And we have seen in detail the inefficiencies and the grave dangers of science—and direction is bound to follow subsidy. Also, we have seen how Federal aid to scientific education is self-defeating.

9. What Should Government Do To Encourage Scientific Research and Development?

What, then, should the government do, if anything, to encourage research and development? We have repeatedly outlined the recommended principles of government policy: to avoid interfering positively in the free market or in scientific inquiry, and confine itself to changing the provisions of its own rules and laws that hamper free scientific research. The latter category, however, leaves room for far more government action than one might think.

Some of the recommended policies which flow from these basic principles have already been outlined:

(1) Shift military research and development from governments to private contracts.

(2) Pay market wages for scientists used by government or government-contracts.

(3) Relax civil service red tape, to provide merit payment and promotions.

(4) Remove undue security regulations and red tape on government-contracted scientific work.

(5) Remove Atomic Energy Commission regulations and subsidies of the atomic energy industry.

(6) Encourage state governments to shift from truly regressive, "progressive education" in the public schools to solid educations in subject matter, to repeal compulsory attendance, and educationist requirements that restrict the supply of good teachers, and to substitute merit payment for the uniformities of civil service regulation.

(7) Encourage state governments to repeal rate regulation of the public industry.

But there is another broad category of worthy government action on which we have not touched: tax exemptions. Taxes cripple free energies, productive work and investment. The best way for government to encourage free activity in any area is to remove its own tax burdens on that area. Contrary to common belief, a tax exemption is not simply equivalent to a government subsidy. For a subsidy mulcts taxpayers in order to give a special grant to the favored party. It thereby adds to the ratio of government activity in the economy, distorts productive resources, and multiples the dangers of government control and repression. A tax exemption, or any other type of tax reduction, on the other hand, reduces the ratio of government to private action; it frees private energies and allows them to develop unhampered; it reduces the danger of government control and distortion of the economy. It is a step toward the free market and the free society, just as a government subsidy is a step away from the free society.

Another point about tax exemption: it avoids many of the problems entailed by government subsidy in deciding which particular firms and locations should obtain the grant. Should government concentrate its funds on a few large universities or medical schools, for example, or should tax funds be distributed pro-rata to each of the various states, or should they be used to help the poor states catch up to the wealthy?[54] There is no rational way to decide this problem, and thus end aggravating conflicts between different groups in society. These conflicts and problems can be avoided by simply lowering taxes, and allowing free individuals and the free market to decide where and how they will allocate their funds.

Here are some examples of the many constructive things government can do, via tax exemptions and reductions, to encourage scientific progress in America:

(1) Tax Credits to business corporations for contributions to colleges and universities for scientific research. This will stimulate

[54]Thus, see Gellhorn, *Medical Research: A Mid Century Survey*, p. 145.

basic research in its proper place: in colleges and universities. (Also recommended by National Science Foundation)

(2) Tax Credits to Individuals on income tax for contributions to scientific research in colleges and universities. (Recommended by National Science Foundation)

(3) Making Tax Deductible, Expenses by Business in training scientists at universities. (Recommended by National Science Foundation)

(4) Making Tax Deductible, Contributions by Business to individual scientific research.

(5) Making Educational Expenses (for science or other higher education) Tax Deductible on Parents' income taxes.

(6) Permitting individual scientists and investors to Average Their Incomes over many years, for Income tax purposes.

(7) Lowering Corporation Income Tax rates, to permit more investment in research and development.

(8) Lowering Individual Income Taxes, especially in the Upper Brackets, to permit

greater investment of private risk capital in new inventions.

(9) Permitting Amortization of Equipment at any time pattern the owner wishes, thus allowing rapid amortization of new, innovatory projects.

(10) Lowering, or Repealing, Federal and State Inheritance Taxes, to permit much more private risk capital in new inventions.

(11) Lowering the Capital Gains Tax on Individuals—to stimulate research and development of inventions, which can be sold as capital assets for capital gains.

(12) Lowering the Capital Gains Tax on Corporations—to permit corporations to try to pile up new inventions in order to increase their assets, and therefore increase the total market value of their securities.

10.
AUTOMATION

IN ALL OF THE PROBLEMS discussed above, the charge has been that free market activity was deficient in some form of scientific research of development. In the question of automation, the charge is really the reverse: that technological improvement might become so great as to threaten dire consequences, particularly unemployment.

Now the spectre of "technological unemployment" has been with us at least since the early days of the Industrial Revolution, when benighted workers smashed machines which came to create jobs for them and raise their standards of living immeasurably above the subsistence level. Despite all manner of refutation, it recurs continually, the latest manifestation being the fashionable view that the current chronic unemployment during a recovery is caused by "too much" increase in productivity (when it is really caused by excessive union wage rates). It is about time that this absurd notion of technological unemployment be laid to rest once and for all. Who was displaced by the steam shovel? How many millions of ditch diggers are now out of work because of it? Where are the billions of unemployed that are supposed to have been caused by the replacement of the human pack animal by the wagon and the truck? Where are they, if the doctrine of technological unemployment is correct? Where are the millions of unemployed resulting from the Industrial Revolution—when the truth is the other way round, that thousands of beggars had nothing to do until the Industrial Revolution rescued them!

Actually, a technological improvement in an industry has the following result: if the demand for the product is elastic (and approximately half of the products have an elastic demand), then the lower prices, and lower costs, of the product will stimulate increased demand and increased production, expanding employment in the industry. If the demand is inelastic, then the improvement will cause less resources to be devoted to the industry, and lower employment; but since prices have declined, the consumers take the funds that they had formerly spent on this industry and spend them elsewhere, thus generating more employment in the other industries. One of the "other industries" that will be expanded will be the industry of making the new machines or new products. Thus: there is no technological unemployment remaining. Automation will have the same effect as any technological improvement, expanding employment in some industries, contracting them in others—but leaving no residue of technological unemployment.[55]

Discussing the problem of technological unemployment, the Earl of Halsbury writes that he knows of no instance where technological progress has caused prolonged

---

[55]This, indeed, is the effect of any change in the economy, whether of consumer wants, of natural resources, of climate, or technology: employment in some firms and industries will be expanded, and in others will be contracted.

unemployment, or, indeed, where technological regression has caused unemployment![56]

More specifically on automation, it is expected to increase the demand for skilled workers in industry, and decrease demand for the unskilled, who can shift (thus continuing recent pro-automation trends) into the service trades, which cannot be automated. Halsbury estimated that practically no unemployment, even temporarily, need be involved in such shifting, since there is a 2 percent "natural" turnover in industry per annum, due to retirement of old and recruiting of young workers, and that the redeployment of labor caused by automation will not be nearly at heavy at this rate. The retirement-recruitment process will therefore be a good buffer against even temporary unemployment. Argyle adds that there is even greater room for mobility, for in addition to this process, about 10 percent of workers leave per annum for other

[56]The Earl of Halsbury, "Introduction," in E.M. Hugh-Jones, ed., *The Push-Button World* (University of Oklahoma Press, 1956).

reasons and that these too will buffer against forced unemployment.[57]

Many of the semi-skilled, and even the unskilled, workers will be upgraded from routine, assembly-line type jobs into better paying, more skilled and varied work. It is largely the routine work that will be eliminated. In many instances, automation will not even decrease the workers in the specific jobs affected. Thus, Halsbury estimates that computerized accountancy, which will permit cheaper and more economic calculation of payrolls, and faster inventory and stock control, will also open up and partially solve a range of new problems, which firms couldn't even have thought of tackling before: such as "production scheduling." As a result, he predicts that as many accountants will need to be employed a generation hence as now, except that they will need more skills than they require now.

Automation will be largely applicable, and certainly only economically applicable, in the

[57]Michael Argyle, "Social Aspects of Automation," in ibid., p. 113.

mass production industries, such as manufacturing, electrical goods, office machinery. It will be feasible for small-scale firms (the new "numerical control") as well as large in these areas. There will still be plenty of room, however, for homemade goods, crafts, services of persons, etc. And Woollard warns against wild overestimation of what automation in manufacturing will amount to:

> if by the term "automatic factory" one is tempted to think of a plant in which the materials are loaded at the beginning of the week, then everyone goes home to play golf expecting to come in on Saturday morning to find the work loading itself on trucks for dispatch, the automatic factory is just a pipe-dream. I doubt very much whether we shall ever see anything of the sort.[58]

In addition, such industries as transportation and retailing do not seem to be adapted to automation. And Spencer estimates that office automation, while requiring considerable retraining

---

[58]Frank G. Woollard, "Automation in Engineering Production," in ibid., p. 38.

and upgrading of office staff, will not lead to any overall reduction in clerical labor. Office needs for labor have been steadily increasing, due to increased complexity of industry, and the effect of computers will be to stop or slow down this growth, rather than actually unemploy any large number of clerical staff; it will reduce considerably the drudgery of present clerical work.[59]

Rational optimism about the employment effects of automation has been well expressed by H.R. Nicholas, one of Britain's most prominent trade union leaders. Nicholas points out that automation creates employment, that our present-day technology has been a boon, rather than a handicap, to employment. Nicholas points out that the numbers employed in our presently most automated industries, such as petroleum, have expanded rather than contracted, because of the prosperity of the industry. There has been more work for tankers, railroads, trucks, etc., to move oil, for shipyards to build these tankers, for managerial, sales, maintenance help

[59]W.R. Spencer, "Administrative Applications of Automation," in ibid., p. 107.

in the industry: none of whom will be displaced by automation.[60]

One point about automation that should not be overlooked:

> it will greatly improve the safety of industrial work, many of the unsafe jobs (such as handling atomic, fissionable materials) being automatically accomplished.[61]

Let us, therefore, put aside the old Luddite (machine-wrecking) bogeyman of technological unemployment, and hail modern developments of automation for what it is and will be: a superb method of greatly increasing the standards of living and the leisure hours, of all of us. We can therefore, hail the Douglas Subcommittee when it reported as follows:

---

[60]H.R. Nicholas, "The Trade Union Approach to Automation," in ibid.

[61]See *Automation and Technological Change, Report of the Subcommittee on Economic Stabilization to the Joint Committee of the Economic Report* (Washington, D.C.: 1955), p. 6.

> One highly gratifying thing which appeared throughout the hearings was the evidence that all elements in the American economy accept and welcome progress, change, and increasing productivity. This flexibility of mind and temperament has been a conspicuous characteristic of American industry for generations in well-known contrast to that of many other countries. Not a single witness raised a voice in opposition to automation and advancing technology. This was true of the representatives of organized labor as well as of those who spoke from the side of management. ... Labor, of course, recognizes that automatic machinery lessons the drudgery for the individual worker and contributes greatly to the welfare and standard of living of all.[62]

[62]Ibid., pp. 4–5.

Epilogue:

The Values of Technology

There is a wing of opinion, here and abroad, that is positively opposed to modern technology and all it stands for, believing that mode and technology brutalizes man, enslaves and "depersonalizes" him, ruins his culture, etc.[63]

Fortunately, this view is overwhelmingly rejected by the bulk of our nation, and therefore there is no need to enter into extended refutation here. But it might be apropos to cite the

[63]Thus, see Ralph Ross and Ernest Van den Haag, *The Fabric of Society, and Introduction to the Social Sciences* (New York: Harcourt, Brace, and Cox, 1957).

views of this subject of two social philosophers with very different views on other matter:

Thus, Professor Ernest Nagel, of the Department of Philosophy, of Columbia University:

> it is by no means evident that a life of deep satisfaction and dedication to the values of a liberal civilization is enjoyed by a smaller fraction of American society than of other types of culture, whether present or past. Critics of American mass culture tend to forget that only comparatively small elite groups in the great civilizations of the past were privileged to share in the high achievements of those cultures. ... In our own society, on the other hand, modern science and technology have made available to unprecedented numbers the major resources of the great literatures and the arts of the past and present, never accessible before in such variety even to the societies. ... The evidence seems to me overwhelming that the growth of scientific intelligence has helped to bring about not only improvements in the material circumstances

> of life, but also an enhancement in its quality.[64]

And here Father Bernard W. Dempsey, of the Institute of Social Order:

> There are those who see in the mechanization of modern industry an inevitable and devastating anti-personal force. ... First of all, man has been condemned to earn his bread in the sweat of his brow; and yet past ages have more sweat and less bread than typical American industrial workers experience. ... Finally, the industrial discipline can also be challenging, interesting and inspiring, especially when an able mechanic is furnished good tools and materials to work with. We must not forget that the farmer is weather-paced, season-paced and animal-paced with a tyranny that is at least as exacting as the industrial discipline. ... In the day of serfs in Western Europe the horse was the symbol of nobility and knighthood. Many American workers in the course of a day control more horse

---

[64]Ernest Nagel, "The Place of Science in a Liberal Education," *Daedalus* (Winter, 1959): 66–67.

> power than there was on the whole field of Agincourt.[65]

[65]Bernard W. Dempsey, S.J., "The Worker As Person," *Review of Social Economy* (March, 1954): 19–20.

Index

The Mises Institute, founded in 1982, is a teaching and research center for the study of Austrian economics, libertarian and classical liberal political theory, and peaceful international relations. In support of the school of thought represented by Ludwig von Mises, Murray N. Rothbard, Henry Hazlitt, and F.A. Hayek, we publish books and journals, sponsor student and professional conferences, and provide online education. Mises.org is a vast resource of free material for anyone in the world interested in these ideas.

Mises Institute
518 West Magnolia Avenue
Auburn, Alabama 36830
mises.org

Made in the USA
Monee, IL
13 September 2026

62976957R00075